KILLHOPE WHEEL
by Jon Silkin

for Carol
from Jon
Durham 8.12.79

THE MID NORTHUMBERLAND ARTS GROUP 1971

North Now Pamphlet No. 3

SBN 9501109 22
Published 1971 by
The Mid Northumberland Arts Group (MidNAG)
Ashington, Northumberland,
England.
Price 60p. ($1.20)

Reprinted 1975
Produced by Litho Services, Newcastle upon Tyne

Tree

Under the yard, earth could enable nothing, nothing
opened in it. I smelt it once, when the floor
was up, disabled, rank. I made boxes
and grow mint, rhubarb, parsley
and seedlings that lift a furl of leaves, slightly
aside an unwavering stem.
A friend dragged a barrel off rocks, we took it home;
I chose a tree for it. It is five foot
with branches that may stretch across
the wall, with minute fruits, of hardly any colour.
Its leaves point open, and down. The whole tree
can glisten, or die. It is dark green
in earth mixed with peat dug by a lake
and dung I crumbled in.
I can't fudge up a relationship, but it gladdens
you, as the sun concentrates it, and I
want the creature for what it is
to live beyond me.

(untitled)

Small hills, among the fells, come apart from the large
where streams drop; the water-flowers
bloom at the edges, or in the shallows, together,
and are white. Whoever comes here, comes, glad, at least
and as they look, it is with some care, you can feel
that on flower, may tree, or dry-stone wall
their gaze collects in a moist, comely pressure.
I feel this, but slog elsewhere.
Swan Hunter's is where we build naval craft;
they emerge: destroyer, the submarine
fitted, at length, by electricians. Their work
is inspected; it is again re-wired. In the heat
men walk high in the hulk on planks, one
of them tips, and he falls the depth of the hold.
It is hot. The shithouses are clagged, the yard's
gates closed for security. The food is not good.
Some people in here are maimed.
I am trying to make again the feeling
plants have, and each creature has, looked at,
demure, exultant. The man who has fallen
looks at me, and looks away

Centering

At the West End, a bridge.
Coaling houses, shutes, and among such power,
contrived, at the top, a little lever
which would unclasp the heavy trap.
All the ships come for here is fuel. Few come.
And none, further.
Near the bridge, each side, houses
struggling to cross over.

More east, seawards, a further bridge.
The trains bend that way, then, turning square,
cross the whole river.
Below, the quay, meant to focus
activity to it.

The maritime offices, craft
moored from Denmark.
The masts' shadows stable on the customs sheds.

No centre can be formed
here or by the next bridge. The trains
pass on a tier above the road.

Nor here; the road belts between
the strength of the region fused into two spans,
gone.

Two precipitate banks, where water pushes
within a moment of the quick of you, bituminous
and rank.
If you were made
at the river-side
you have to be a spanning, at least.

Killhope Wheel
1860
County Durham

1860. Killhope Wheel, cast
forty feet in iron across, is swung
by water off the North Pennines
washing lead ore crushed here.

And mined, here. Also fluor-spar.
In 1860 soldiers might kill
miners if they struck.

A board says that we're free to come in.
Why should it seem absurd to get
pain from such permission? Why have

I to see red coat soldiers prick
between washed stones, and bayonets
tugged from the seeping flesh?

Among the north pennines what might
have opened the flesh of miners, who chucked
their tools aside?

I can't work out what I have
come here for; there's no mineable lead
or work of that kind here now.

Why does a board, tacked to wood,
concerning my being free to visit
give my useless pain nourishment?

Like water. I am its water, dispersed
in the ground I came from; and have footage
on these hills, stripped of lead,

which the sheep crop, insensibly white.
The mist soaks their cries into them.

Strike

The earth comes moist-looking, and blackens;
a trickle of earth where the feet pressed,
twice a day, wearing off the grass.
Where the miners
were seen: a letter blown damply
into the corner of a hut: "Oh dear love, come to me"
and nothing else.

Where are they?
The sheep bleat back to the mist balding
with terror; where
are they? The miners
are under the ground.

A pale blue patch of thick worsted
a scrag of cotton;
the wheel is still that washed the pounded ore.
They were cut down.

Almost turned by water, a stammer of the huge wheel
groping at the bearings.
Their bayonets; the red coat
gluey with red.

The water shrinks
to its source. The wheel,
in balance.

Spade

George Culley, Isaac Greener?

A want of sound hangs
in a drop of moisture from the wheel that
turned and washed the ore.

A rustling of clothes on the wind. The water does not move.

I have come here to be afraid.
I came for love to bundle
what was mine. I am scared
to sneak into the hut to find your coat.

When you put down your pick,
when others wouldn't sprag
the mine's passages; when you said no:

soldiers, who do not strike,
thrust
their bayonets into you.

They were told to.

The young mayor, shitting, closeted
with chain on his neck. I want to

push my hands into your blood
because I caused you to use yours.

I did not die; love, I did not. All the parts
of England fell melting like lead away,
as you showed me the melting once, when you and the men
with you were jabbed,

and without tenderness, were filled over;
no psalm, leaf-like, shading the eyelid
as the eye beneath is dazed abruptly
in the earth's flare of black light
burning after death.

The spade digging in the sunlight illuminates the face of my God.
Blind him.

(untitled)

Concerning strength,
it is unequal. In a paddock
by Stakeford, slag, with bushes dripping
over stone, a horse crops, slowly, his strength
tethered into the ground. The Wansbeck
shivers over the stone, bits of coal, and where
it halts a pool fills, oily
and twitching. Closer to the sea, it drops
under a bridge, coming to ground
where the mind opens, and gives uselessly to
the sun such created heat the air
cleaves to the flesh,
the bench facing the water, sat on by old men.
If this goes, nothing: this clearness
which draws a supple smell through old skin
making a pause for it. Houses and scrap will heap,
and flake, as
if organs of the soil clagged
with shreddings of rust.

Platelayer

(*for J.M.*)

'I did not serve, but was skilled
for fifty years, laying plates
measured as carefully apart
as seedlings.' The line came
west from Morpeth, crossing
the third road for Scotland.
At Knowesgate, four houses
group on a bank, set away.
A station was built there.
'I laid plates for eight miles,
but short of Morpeth, sledging chucks
that held the rails; kept them so,
although this has gone now.
Yet here are four pines of
the five I put in. And here
I helped to concrete that
that was the goods bay.
My dog has sixteen years.
We both suffer the heat.
And yet her owners had said
that she must be put down.
I did not say that. And the lupins
strike through the platform;
with a better chance they'd have not
done well, I think.
But what I think is that
my work was finished up: five years
past the track taken apart.

No, not so; now we've cranes
to hoist the lengths that we
laid down, form on form. Also gone
a certain friend, who finished
when I was made free.
I shan't work any job
twice. And this is strange,
having the letter from the man,
although it was not him.
Yet surely as like him
as the bolts drove in.
"I can't think of your name
or what you are. You must
excuse me and I have
nothing to tell you and
why I am shut up here
I can't speak of with nothing
to speak about."
But still I am certain
the track we built was skilled,
although you can't tell that.'

Acknowledgements

Some of these poems have appeared previously in *Here Now, The Review, Stand, Times Literary Supplement* and *Tribune.* Others have been broadcast on the BBC's *Poetry Now.*

The cover photograph is reproduced by kind permission of the North of England Open-Air Museum.

These poems appeared in *The Principle of Water* by Jon Silkin, published by Carcanet Press in 1974.